DODGE BROTHERS

D1571722

STILLWATE
EMERGEN
24 HR ROAD SERVICE
STILLWATER
GARAGE
DU·3·5660

DODGE
PICKUP TRUCKS

Steve Statham

Motorbooks International
Publishers & Wholesalers

First published in 1998 by Motorbooks International Publishers & Wholesalers, 729 Prospect Avenue, PO Box 1, Osceola, WI 54020-0001 USA

Library of Congress Cataloging-in-Publication Data
Statham, Steve.
Dodge pickup trucks/Steve Statham.
p. cm.—(Enthusiast color series)
Includes index.
ISBN 0-7603-0350-9 (paperback: alk. paper)
1. Dodge trucks—History. 2. Dodge trucks—Pictorial works.
I. Title. II. Series.
TL230.5.D63S73 1998
629.224—dc21 97-43446

On the front cover: With the new Ram, Dodge managed to suggest the classic look of a 1940s-era pickup, like Brian Webb's 1948 B-1-B, while creating a thoroughly modern truck. John and Marilyn Cornfoot own the 1995 Ram 1500.

On the frontispiece: The Dodge Brothers logo graces the radiator grille on this 1918 screenside commercial car.

On the title page: Dodge's Power Wagon earned its reputation for toughness on the battlefields of World War II. A no-frills rig designed for hard work, a Power Wagon could take just about any abuse an owner could dish out. Frank Naugle owns this beautifully restored 1948 example.

On the back cover: Fire-engine red paint, brightwork under the hood, and those towering chrome exhaust stacks made Dodge's Li'l Red Truck a hip cruiser in the late 1970s. This mint 1978 belongs to John and Marilyn Cornfoot.

Printed in Hong Kong through World Print, Ltd.

Contents

Preface and Acknowledgments

My first Dodge truck was a Dodge Deora. Okay, so it was only a Hot Wheels toy, and both the Deora and the two tiny plastic surfboards it came with are *long* gone. But that 1967 show car and the toys it inspired revealed a healthy spark of creativity among Dodge people, a creativity that certainly caught my young imagination. Lately, that creativity at Dodge has been sparked again, and this time it's not just fanciful concept trucks doing the sparking. Dodge has been putting some bold truck ideas on the street, and the public has responded as if they had been waiting their entire lives for an alternative to the hordes of Ford and Chevy pickups so prevalent on the world's highways. Hence, this book.

The author's 1984 Dodge Rampage 2.2 on the Pacific Coast Highway, 1985. It was a hell of a drive, and whatever faults the Rampage may have had, it could carve a road like few other pickups.

Of course, sometimes creativity can be overrated. My second Dodge truck was a 1984 Rampage 2.2, and although it served me well enough, it may have been a bit *too* creative a variation on the pickup truck theme. It was the only American-made, front-wheel drive, four-cylinder truck, and thus was always a bit of an odd duck. On the plus side, it handled well, was quick for a four-cylinder, and was a unique vehicle at a time when cars and trucks were looking more and more alike. I was proud of it when I drove it off the lot.

On the negative side, it was somewhat flimsy, had an awkward steering wheel position, and didn't hold a lot of cargo. It was cheap enough to buy, but suffered from that dreaded New Chrysler Corporation disease of the 1980s: depreciation syndrome. And upon seeing it for the first time, one woman I was dating curled back her lips in a Texas sneer and said "That's not a *truck*!"

Since then I have driven Dodge's turbo diesels, V-10s, V-8 Sport models, stripped trucks, old trucks, and competitors of all sorts. I feel confident in saying these are the "good old days" for Dodge. As I'll get to later in this book, the 1994 Ram has revitalized the Dodge truck line like few other vehicles in the company's history. That halo effect has even started to get people interested in the older Dodge trucks, and original parts are drying up just as fast as prices are rising.

Steering wheel detail, 1957 Dodge Sweptside.

Fortunately, all this activity has generated a lot of enthusiasm for the trucks, and the network of Dodge owners and experts has grown rapidly. Many of these people deserve my sincere gratitude, because without their help this book would be mostly blank pages. I'd like to start by thanking DeAnna Weber with Dodge Truck Motorsport for contributing photography of the NASCAR Craftsman Truck racers. Monty Montgomery with the D100 Sweptside Registry was a great help with general information and bird-dogging suitable trucks, and here's hoping he gets his 1978 440-powered D150 back on the road in the near future.

As editor of *Mopar Muscle* magazine, Greg Rager has been a treasure-trove of facts, tidbits, and good ideas, not to mention photography. Thanks, Greg, for all your help. Another new magazine friend is Patrick Ertel at *This Old Truck* magazine, who graciously cracked open his photo files and contributed some good photography of several hard-to-find trucks, like Tom Luttrull's 1946 Dodge. So did Karl Pippart III and his Classic Auto Research Service, and Don Althaus of Lake Havasu City, Arizona. Alvin Garcia and everyone else associated with the Hays Antique Truck Museum in Woodland, California, were of great assistance and deserve special thanks for providing photography of the museum's 1930 Dodge Model U1-A 1/2-ton screen side. I must also acknowledge the valuable reference works of Don Bunn, Tom Brownell, and John Gunnell, such as *The Standard Catalog of American Light Duty Trucks* and *Dodge Pickups History and Restoration Guide 1918-1971.* These works have provided much useful and hard-to-find information.

Finally, I must thank all those truck owners who graciously allowed me to photograph their vehicles. In basic order of appearance: Roy Brister, Sacramento, California, 1918 Dodge Brothers Screen side; Gene Byrne, Broomfield, Colorado, 1936 Dodge LE-15 fruit truck; Wanda Russell and W. Pat O'Bryan, Brownwood, Texas, 1944 Dodge WC-57 Command Car; Brian Webb, Boerne, Texas, 1948 B1B pickup; Frank Naugle, The Woodlands, Texas, 1948 B1 PW-126 Power Wagon; Roy and Jane Braden, La Vernia, Texas, 1950 Dodge street machine pickup; The Texas Military Forces Museum, Camp Mabry, Austin, Texas (with special thanks to General John C.L. Scribner), 1951 M-37 4x4 3/4-ton military cargo truck; Lloyd Bluntzer, Robstown, Texas, 1952 Power Wagon; Peter Sprouse, Austin, Texas, 1954 C1PW Superior Coach school bus; Lewis E. Hurt, Lampasas, Texas, 1957 Dodge Sweptside (with a *major* portion of gratitude to Randy Peurifoy for his help); John and Marilyn Cornfoot, Kerrville, Texas, 1978 Li'l Red Express and 1995 Ram 1500; Bob Boedeker, Murphy, Texas, 1979 Li'l Red Express (with a tip o' the hat to Richard Elms for his assistance); James Edick, North Syracuse, New York, 1989 Shelby Dakota; Kevin Hines, Special Edition, Inc., Bremen, Indiana, 1996 Ram-side pickups; and Charles Lockett, Cleburne, Texas, 1996 Ram Sport four-door conversion.

—Steve Statham

Kendall
MOTOR
OIL
CRAFTSMAN
Mopar
DODGE
GOODYEAR
29
Mopar
REMAN
PARTS
DODGE
18
DANA
VICTOR REINZ
WIX
DANA
CRAFTSMAN
Cummins
DODGE
DODGE

Introduction
Up by the Bootstraps

The fortunes of Dodge have always been an up and down affair. The original Dodge Brothers cars and pickups were met with tremendous critical acclaim and strong sales, but as part of the Chrysler Corporation, Dodge has usually been the distant third-place follower of Ford and General Motors. There are peaks in Dodge truck history where a rugged reputation and handsome styling helped make the trucks competitive, and some pretty deep valleys where quality control lapsed and styling was either too aged or too ugly to generate much interest. For too many years, a Dodge truck was the choice for people who couldn't afford a Ford.

Up and down. Down and up. One "up" period was after the redesigned and modernized 1972 Dodge D- and W-Series trucks were introduced, but Dodge learned the hard way that if you leave something sitting on the shelf too long—like 22 years—it eventually goes bad. So it was in 1993, when Dodge met the challenge of refined Ford and Chevy offerings with a two-decade-old truck and only 7 percent of the growing full-size pickup market. It had been a long, slow slide.

But then Dodge tossed out the conservative playbook, threw the long ball, and introduced the radical 1994 Ram. The new Ram revitalized the Dodge truck image like few other models in the company's history. The styling was bold. The Ram was larger and had the biggest engines available in a light-duty pickup. And the timing was right, with a rebounding economy and, for once, Ford and Chevy pickups that had started to look a bit stale themselves. As of this writing, Dodge's newest "up" period is still going strong, with no letup in sight.

Of course, the new Ram hasn't been the only Dodge truck with the vitality to capture hearts and pocketbooks. The Li'l Red Express Truck of the late 1970s has gathered steam with collectors. The 1939

Dodge won its last NASCAR Winston Cup race in 1977 and dropped out of NASCAR soon after, giving Mopar fans precious little to cheer about for the next two decades. When the NASCAR SuperTruck Series (later changed to Craftsman Truck Series) was born in 1994, coinciding with the introduction of the new Ram, it provided the perfect arena for competition. Although Ford and Chevy dominated the 1995 and 1996 seasons, the Dodges started pulling into victory lane in 1997. Shown are Bob Keselowski, Jimmy Hensley, Michael Dokken, and Darin Brassfield. *Dodge Motorsport.*

The popularity of Dodge trucks has steadily increased over the years. Even Power Wagons have their own reunions, such as this Texas group in 1997. Other trucks, like the Li'l Red Express Truck of the 1970s, are popular at Mopar musclecar shows.

to 1947 models remain favorites, and the Sweptside trucks of the 1950s are perennial collectibles. During World War II there was great affection for the 4x4 Dodge military vehicles, and the postwar civilian Power Wagons found buyers for two more decades. And the Cummins Turbo Diesels introduced in 1989 almost single-handedly kept Dodge truck sales from imploding.

But the 1994 T-300 Ram was a crucial part of Chrysler's recovery in the 1990s, a major part of the revitalized image America's number three auto maker now enjoys. No other Dodge truck has sold in these volumes. The Ram sold 383,960 units in 1996 alone. The truck has actively lured away Ford and Chevy owners. Its success has given the Dodge team a new strut, and Dodge owners no longer have to make excuses.

The Dodge Ram was one of the top-10 best-selling vehicles in the land in the mid-1990s. Market share increased from less than 7 percent of the full-size truck market in 1993 to nearly 13 percent of the market in 1994, and 15 percent in 1995. The Ram and Dakota pickups are the last stronghold of the V-8 engine family at Chrysler, and arguably the last link to the musclecar glory days of yore. The Ram has even revitalized Chrysler's racing program, with the Craftsman Truck Series race Rams in NASCAR putting the company back in the thick

Dodge never made a four-door, Ram-based, sport utility vehicle, but that hasn't stopped enterprising customizing shops from filling in the gap. The 1994-and-up Ram has revitalized interest in Dodge trucks among the aftermarket industry. The "Ram Sport" pictured is one of about a half-dozen created by Custom Conversions in Cleburne, Texas.

of America's most popular motorsport arena. Through the NASCAR Rams, Richard Petty is once again associated with Dodge, another reminder of past glory.

Also deserving credit for Dodge's turnaround is the mid-size Dakota. Although no sales threat to the Ford Ranger or Chevy S-10 upon its introduction, the Dakota's sales have steadily risen as the truck has been improved. The introduction of the Magnum V-8 engine was the first major shot in the arm. The V-8 was something other compact pickups simply did not offer, and gave Mopar drag racing enthusiasts something they could take to the track on Saturday night. The 1997 Dakota adopted Ram styling, and soon provided the platform for a sport utility vehicle, the 1998 Durango.

All of this helps generate more interest in the older Dodge trucks. Interest in the new builds appreciation for the old, and vice-versa. Many collectors and restoration-minded souls are giving vintage Dodge pickups a second look, and prices for hard-to-find parts have escalated as demand has increased. All of this bodes well for America's number-three auto maker. By building solid, exciting pickups, the company has cast a warm glow over the entire Dodge history, and is making people look eagerly toward the future.

HORSELESS
CARRIAGE

1 Brothers In Industry

As the first century of the automobile's existence draws to a close, it is easy to forget that most of the great names affixed to the nation's cars and trucks belonged to real people, with real lives, who made very real individual contributions to the development of the horseless carriage. Here in the waning years of the twentieth century, new cars and trucks are named by committee, with endless focus groups sorting through a variety of alpha-numeric combinations, animal names, buzz words, jargon, and made-up terms that are supposed to remind us of real words of substance (think *Acura Integra*).

Before marketing was so well developed, men placed their own names on their creations. Henry Ford, Walter P. Chrysler, Ransom E. Olds, Louis Chevrolet, David Dunbar Buick, James Ward Packard and William Doud Packard, Robert Craig Hupp, the Studebaker brothers—all affixed their own names to their automobiles. And so it was with the Dodge brothers, John and Horace. They established one of the great American auto companies, a company that thrives as part of the Chrysler Corporation even today, although here in the twilight of the industrial century few remember the origin of the Dodge line. Most people know of Henry Ford and his humble beginnings, and others might be able to associate Chrysler or Chevrolet with a real person's name, but the creators of Dodge cars and trucks have, for the most part, slid past the public's radar screen.

Eighty or 90 years ago, though, people knew who the Dodge brothers were. In the early days of the automotive industry their reputations were among the best. When they announced they were going to produce their own cars and trucks, it was news of the first order.

Born in Michigan, the brothers seemed destined for careers in the automotive industry. John, born in 1864, and Horace, born four years later, both got an early start on learning the machining trade from their father, who owned a machine shop. As the brothers grew older, their industrial talents became apparent. Eventually, the two moved to Canada and built bicycles plus some minor automotive parts. After returning to Detroit

The first Dodge Brothers truck was the 1918 screen side Commercial Car, with production beginning in October 1917. A panel delivery truck soon followed. Payload was rated at 1,000 pounds.

Roll-down side curtains were standard equipment on the Dodge Brothers screen side Commercial Car. Front and rear suspensions used a single spring on each side, a half elliptic in front, and three-quarter elliptic in the rear. The 15-gallon gas tank was located below the seat.

in 1901, they expanded their production of automotive parts, quickly becoming major suppliers in a rapidly expanding industry.

The Dodge brothers' clients were a Who's Who of the early automotive world. They built transmissions for Ransom E. Olds' cars, and engines and axles for Henry Ford's fledgling company. In fact, Ford offered the brothers a share of his growing empire. The arrangement worked well for several years, and certainly made the Dodge brothers rich men.

It was as suppliers to the larger companies that John and Horace established their reputation for technical innovation, and as producers of parts of outstanding durability. Eventually, though, dissatisfaction with their role in the Ford empire grew, and the brothers decided to take that reputation and transfer it to cars of their own creation—an announcement that caused a considerable stir throughout the industry.

The first Dodge Brothers car was rolled out of the Hamtramck, Michigan, factory on November 14, 1914, with a commercial chassis put into production soon after. The Dodge Brothers car was noteworthy for having the first all-steel body in a mass-produced automobile. The Dodge's four-cylinder engine was more powerful than the low-priced Ford's engine, and the car's solid construction made the Dodge Brothers Model 30-35 an immediate hit.

The eventual production of Dodge Brothers trucks was pushed forward by the military's need for ambulances, troop carriers, and the like in World War I. Dodge had already established a rugged reputation in military circles thanks to Army General John Pershing, who had used a fleet of 1916 Dodge Brothers cars in his skirmish with Mexican revolutionary Pancho Villa and pronounced them fit for duty.

In 1917 the Dodge Brothers produced thousands of heavy-duty vehicles for the military, but also turned out trucks for the general public. The Dodge Brothers 1/2-ton screen side Commercial Car went into production October 18, 1917, as a 1918 model. It sold for $885.

Helping the Dodge's reputation was a powerful and technically advanced engine. The Dodge Brothers' 1918 engine was a four-cylinder, with a 3 7/8x4 1/2-inch bore and stroke that yielded 212 cubic inches of displacement. With a 4.0:1

The 1918 screen side used 25-inch wood-spoke wheels, and 33x4-inch tires. "DB" emblems (Dodge Brothers) were displayed on the wheel centercaps.

The 1918 Dodge four-cylinder powerplant displaced 212 cubic inches and produced 35 horsepower at 2,000 rpm. The engine featured an unusual chain-driven combination starter and generator. Fuel feed came through a Stewart vacuum system, while engine cooling was handled by an 11-quart copper/brass radiator.

EXCEPTIONAL RIDING COMFORT

Travel all day, and the next, and the next. Then you will begin to understand what Dodge Brothers, Inc. have accomplished with their long underslung spring equipment, balloon tires and low-swung body lines.

In touring, the master test of riding ease, Dodge Brothers Motor Car now acquits itself with a distinction you have learned to associate only with vehicles of the largest and most expensive type.

DODGE BROTHERS, INC. DETROIT
DODGE BROTHERS (CANADA) LIMITED
TORONTO, ONTARIO

Early in the Chrysler reign, as with this 1930 1/2-ton screen side, light-duty Dodge trucks were powered by either the 175-ci, 45-horsepower, four-cylinder Plymouth engine or the 208-ci six. The cab still used features introduced with the 1927 Graham Brothers trucks, such as the small, rear quarter-windows. *Hays Antique Truck Museum*

Previous
Early Dodge Brothers advertising, like this piece from 1925, focused on the car's engineering and comfort. Truck ads had similar themes, stressing the vehicle's efficiency and reliability. As with the trucks themselves, advertising was in its infancy, offering mercifully straightforward and hype-free text.

compression ratio, the 212 produced 35 horsepower. Ford's Model T had a smaller engine that produced only 20 horsepower, while Chevrolet 1-ton trucks had a large four-cylinder with competitive horsepower. Backing up the four-cylinder was a three-speed transmission with cone-type clutch. Further distinguishing the 212 was an unusual 12-volt starter/generator combination that provided easier starts than many other vehicles.

The screen side truck was essentially a Dodge Brothers car from the windshield forward, but it used heavier rear springs than those used in the automobiles and had larger tires. The wire screens were removable and roll-down side curtains were standard. Payload was rated at 1,000 pounds.

The 1936 Dodge pickups were completely restyled and treated to several mechanical improvements. This LE-15 3/4-ton truck is fitted with a Hercules box, and outfitted with optional chrome headlamps ($3), grille ($6) and bumpers ($2).

Later in 1918 the Dodge Brothers added a Business Car panel truck—priced $100 higher than the screen side—to its offering of commercial vehicles. Advertising copy for these commercial vehicles was direct but dry, focusing on Dodge's rugged construction. "It is so efficient, so strikingly free from need of repair, and so economical to run, that it constitutes a real asset to any business requiring delivery," ads read. "The haulage cost is unusually low."

The car, Commercial Car, and Business Car were extremely successful for Dodge, and by 1920, the Dodge Brothers were number two in automotive sales in the United States. Unfortunately, John and Horace did not get the opportunity to enjoy that success for long.

New Owners

Both Dodge brothers died in 1920: John in January, then Horace in December. Ownership of the company passed to the brothers' widows, and Frederick Haynes took over as president early in 1921. Although the vehicles and the direction of the company did not change in any fundamental way, a new association that affected the truck business developed.

The Graham Brothers of Evansville, Indiana, had their own truck operation going, using a variety of parts from assorted manufacturers. In 1921 Dodge Brothers entered into an agreement with the Graham Brothers, wherein the Graham Brothers would produce heavy-duty trucks using Dodge engines and other Dodge parts. The trucks (badged as Graham Brothers) would then be sold through Dodge dealers. The Graham Brothers trucks were mostly in the 1-ton or 1 1/2-ton category, with Dodge continuing to build its 1/2-ton screen sides and panel trucks. In 1923 Dodge Brothers trucks were upgraded to 3/4-ton status, and given such styling upgrades as a slanted windshield, outside door handles, and a new steering wheel. In 1924 Graham Brothers became a division of Dodge, handling the construction of all larger trucks.

The early and mid 1920s were a fantastic period for Dodge Brothers cars and trucks, with demand typically running well ahead of the company's production capacity. By the end of 1923 Dodge had produced its one millionth vehicle. Dodge's success pulled the Graham Brothers up as well, and the two companies' products grew more closely intertwined.

Meanwhile, the ownership shuffle continued. In 1925 the Dodge widows sold the corporation to a New York banking syndicate. During this time Robert Graham was given a more influential position in the Dodge hierarchy, which led to all Dodge

All trucks in 1936 finally got doors hinged at the front, replacing the rear-hinged doors used previously on some models. Standard instrumentation included the speedometer, ammeter, fuel gauge, oil pressure gauge, and temperature gauge.

It was during 1936 that the Dodge Brothers name was retired from use, to be replaced by simply "Dodge." The leaping ram hood ornament became a fixture in the 1930s, a feature that would be associated with Dodge for most of the next six decades.

Brothers trucks being marketed and sold as Graham Brothers trucks in 1927 and 1928. The ascendancy of Graham Brothers trucks was short-lived, however, once the newest and final owners took over. On July 30, 1928, the newly-formed Chrysler Corporation acquired the Dodge Brothers operation. Dodge continues as the most important division of the Chrysler Corporation to this day, with the highest sales volumes and largest product lineup.

Walter P. Chrysler had been steadily building his own automotive empire in the late 1920s. Chrysler cut his teeth working for Buick and General Motors from 1910 to 1919, and in the early 1920s for Willys. It was at the Maxwell Motor Corporation, though, that his plans for his own auto company began to unfold. The first Chrysler car was introduced in 1924, to great acclaim, and in 1925 the Chrysler Corporation was born from the ashes of the Maxwell-Chalmers Corporation.

Chrysler automobiles competed in the mid-price field, but in 1928 Chrysler established the Plymouth car line as a low-priced competitor for Ford and Chevrolet. One of the advantages of acquiring Dodge for the relatively new Chrysler Corporation (besides Dodge's great reputation) was the Dodge Brothers' extensive network of dealers.

Chrysler had his own ideas for the Dodge truck line, and in 1929 the Graham Brothers name was dropped from the corporate roster. The late 1920s were years of rapid transitions for Dodge truck, with many substantial changes to the product line as Chrysler and Dodge merged. The 208-ci, 58-horsepower six-cylinder was introduced in 1928 for the 1929 model year, and the 1929 Plymouth's four-cylinder engine was phased into the Dodge truck lineup later that year. The Plymouth four-

The 1936 Dodge six produced 70 horsepower from its 201 cubic inches of displacement. The compression ratio was 5.8:1. The oil-bath air cleaner pictured was a $2.50 option.

cylinder displaced 175 cubic inches and produced 45 horsepower at 2,800 rpm. It would become the base light-duty engine through 1933.

Dodge truck brakes were also upgraded after they joined Chrysler Corporation, with some of the larger trucks receiving hydraulic brakes in 1928. By 1929 all Dodge trucks were outfitted with hydraulic stoppers, beating a recalcitrant Henry Ford, and others, to the punch by several years.

Fargo trucks were also introduced during 1928. The Fargo line was a further embodiment of Walter P. Chrysler's desire to expand into every automotive market. The Fargos were initially a separate commercial vehicle line, then a fleet sales division, before becoming a line of export pickups. Many people around the world learned of Chrysler Corporation's products through the Fargo name, particularly Canadians. The Fargo name was used on export trucks through 1972.

The first major styling changes for the Dodge Brothers trucks under Chrysler ownership came for 1933. The 1933 light-duty models were given the sloping grille and swooping fenders so prevalent in 1930s-era automotive design, plus the leaping ram hood ornament that quickly became a Dodge trademark. The 201-ci, flathead six-cylinder offered in 1933 was more powerful than previous sixes. A larger 218-ci six was worked into the lineup in 1934 in 3/4-ton and 1-ton trucks. The 218 eventually became the standard workhorse in Dodge trucks, and survived (in larger displacements) into the 1960s under 1-ton Power Wagon hoods.

Brothers No More

As automakers struggled for new sales during the Great Depression, styling changes were frequent. Dodge cars and trucks were no exception to this practice, and in 1936 Dodge trucks were given another new look. The protruding new grille was now concave instead of convex, featuring multiple vertical grille bars. The series of vertical vents along the hood sides was replaced by a much narrower band of vents that ran from the grille to the cab. The truck sat on a new frame and all cabs finally got front-hinged doors. Prices on these LC-Series trucks started at a Depression-friendly $370 for a chassis and cowl, and $500 for a pickup.

One of the most radically styled trucks of all time also emerged from Dodge in the mid-1930s, the Airflow series. For 1934 Chrysler introduced the dramatically rounded and smoothed Airflow cars, and their influence was transferred to a new truck line later that year as 1935 models. The Airflow cars, with their cascading, waterfall grilles and hunched backs, never caught on with the public, and the Airflow trucks were produced in small numbers, too. The four-ton Airflow trucks were built until 1940 and were mostly bodied as tankers.

Sometime around 1936, as the memories of John and Horace Dodge receded further into the background and the company became more a product of Chrysler planning, the Dodge Brothers nameplate vanished from the sides of pickup hoods. It was replaced by a simple Dodge emblem.

Grille revisions in 1937 and 1938 kept the Dodge pickup fresh, although sales in 1938 still suffered a Depression hangover. One new development was the introduction of a Plymouth line of light-duty trucks to the corporate roster. As early as 1930, Chrysler's price-beater line had offered a Commercial Sedan based on the Plymouth auto. But for 1937 Plymouth offered a real pickup on a real truck chassis. It was, of course, a Dodge in Plymouth clothing, but it allowed Plymouth dealers to have a truck of their own to sell. True to its price-leading position in the corporate hierarchy, the 1937 Plymouth pickup sold for a few dollars less than the Dodge pickup.

The Plymouth pickup had its own grille features and markings, and was powered by the 201-ci, six-cylinder, with its 70 horsepower at 3,000 rpm. The Plymouth trucks were updated as the Dodge trucks were, with the close family resemblance remaining evident throughout the life of the

After World War II the prewar Dodge pickup was put back into production largely unchanged. The 1946 truck, as shown, was introduced to the public with seats redesigned for greater comfort, and increased axle capacities for better durability. The 1946 1/2-ton pickups were still available in a variety of configurations: chassis and cab, chassis and cowl, pickup, canopy truck, and panel truck. *This Old Truck*

line. Plymouth trucks and commercial vehicles were produced into 1942. After the war the Plymouth name would not be found on another truck until the 1970s.

For many collectors, 1939 was the year when Dodge put together its best-looking truck of the decade. The 1939-1947 models featured handsome, art deco-type styling, keeping with the art, architecture, and industrial design styles of the decade. Horizontal grille openings intersected with a plunging chrome trim piece, and the split, two-piece windshield swept back at an aerodynamic angle. Small, horizontal ridges on the fenders mimicked the bold grille design.

Functionally, the new 1939 TC-Series 1/2-ton trucks were powered by the 201-ci six, while the 3/4-ton and 1-ton trucks were powered by the Dodge car's 218-ci six. The trucks had longer springs, improved brakes, a new axle design, and larger fuel tanks. The redesigned dashboard placed the instruments in front of the driver, instead of in the center of the dash.

After a dismal 1938, truck sales were way up for 1939. That year also saw the opening of the huge Dodge truck plant in Warren, Michigan. Little did the movers and shakers at Dodge know, however, the Warren plant would soon have an exclusive customer—the U.S. military.

From 1942 to 1945 Dodge trucks were built almost solely for military use, with only a few thousand built and sold to vital civilian industries (see chapter two). After World War II, the prewar civilian trucks were put back in production (now labeled the WC-Series) with few changes. The trucks that were introduced in 1939 once again rolled out of factories starting in late 1945. Still, the effects of the war were felt. The 1945 models were sold without chrome bumpers, hubcaps, and trim, as chrome was still considered an essential material for the war effort. However, suspensions and axles were beefed up on these postwar pickups.

With the end of the war, stability returned to the auto industry, more or less. The general public snapped up cars and trucks as fast as the industry could build them, which wasn't as fast as the auto makers might have liked due to sporadic material shortages and labor disputes. The WC and WD Dodge trucks were kept in production until 1947, after which, having served their country well, they were retired in favor of a new line of B-series pickups for 1948.

The 1947 pickups, as pictured, were virtually unchanged from the 1946 models. The leaping-ram hood ornament of the 1930s had been replaced in 1941 by a much more stylized figure that was still suggestive of a ram's head—if you squinted. When the new trucks arrived for 1948, they again utilized a recognizable ram hood ornament. *This Old Truck*

POWER WAGON

2 Wheels of War and Power

The bombing of Pearl Harbor on December 7, 1941, mobilized America as never before. With Imperial Japanese troops spreading through the Pacific Rim and German troops advancing steadily throughout Europe, it was evident that a total national effort would have to be made to fight such a major war on two fronts. Government agencies like the Office of Defense Transportation (ODT) suspended civilian car and truck production, instituted rationing of gas and tires, and reduced speed limits. Civilian truck production at Dodge shut down on April 30, 1942. Civilian automobile production had shut down two months earlier.

It was natural that Dodge would be called upon to be a primary producer of trucks, weapons carriers, and command cars in the second World War, because the company had done such a noteworthy job producing trucks in the first World War. The company that produced so many military screen sides, pickups, and ambulances in World War I was soon busy producing all manner of trucks in the second. Like America's other automakers, the Dodge factories even diversified into building such items as bomber engines, shell casings, tank parts, and anti-aircraft parts. But it was through trucks that most uniformed men came to recognize Dodge's war contributions.

Dodge built 255,196 military 4x4 trucks of all types during World War II. The earliest war vehicles were the 1/2-ton 4x4 VC-Series in 1940. The six different VC vehicles used recognizable Dodge sheet metal from the existing pickups, although they were stronger than ordinary trucks under the skin. The VCs were built as pickups, command cars, weapons carriers, and carryalls.

The Dodge trucks that are most associated with World War II, however, are the WC-Series produced from late 1940 until 1945. These trucks had new, rugged-looking sheet metal and were built in a dizzying array of body styles and chassis configurations. Although the WC pickups used the same cab as the prewar civilian trucks, there was no mistaking the two. The WCs had a large, aggressive

With an intimidating name that perfectly fit Dodge's intimidating truck, the Power Wagon was arguably the burliest, most rugged American pickup available at any price. The civilian Power Wagons were sold in the U.S. until 1968, although the name lived on affixed to another generation of Dodge four-wheel-drive trucks.

grille opening, tapered snouts and wide fenders with huge wheel openings.

The WC trucks all used 218-ci sixes or—for most later, larger models—the 230-ci flathead six. A few WC-Series trucks were built as 4x2 panel trucks, but the vast majority were 4x4 trucks. These utilized a one-speed transfer case and full-floating rear axle.

Later in the war even 6x6 cargo trucks were produced in the WC-Series, the WC-62 and WC-63. These open-cab trucks used a two-speed transfer case, and were mostly used as weapons carriers. More than 43,000 of these 6x6 trucks were built, in addition to the more than 250,000 4x4 vehicles.

The most numerous of the WC-Series Dodge vehicles, though, were 3/4-ton 4x4 weapons carriers. Versatile and rugged, this design provided the base for civilian Power Wagons in the postwar years. The WC-type trucks also saw duty in the Korean War and at various cold-war spots around the globe.

The 1944 WC-57 command car was one of the 3/4-ton military WC-Series trucks that helped win the war. The command cars were used largely for reconnaissance or transporting officers, although these vehicles had 101 different uses. The WC-57 rode on a 98-inch wheelbase, the stubbiest length used on the WC vehicles. Production of the WC-57 totaled 6,010 during the war years.

The military command cars wasted little space. The trunk held items such as tools, shovels and, likely, spare weapons.

The machine gun mount on the WC-57 was located along the passenger side of the dash. Other configurations of the World War II-vintage WC-Series trucks could accommodate larger guns, in the 37-mm range, in the bed.

The military WC vehicles of World War II relied on the 230-ci flathead six-cylinder, which produced 92 horsepower at 3,200 rpm. The six was backed by a four-speed transmission. The four-wheel-drive system used a one-speed transfer case.

Civilian Power Wagons were given the bare essentials for heavy-duty work, and not much else. Front shock absorbers were standard equipment for this 1948 B-1-PW, but the rear shocks were optional. The suspension featured multiple leaf springs stacked together as thick as a railroad tie: 14 leaves in the rear, 11 in front.

The last of the military-exclusive Dodge trucks was the Korean era M-37. A further development of the military WC 3/4-ton 4x4 chassis, the M-37 went into production in 1950 and was built until 1954, and then again from 1957 to 1963. It rode on a 112-inch wheelbase, and was powered by the 230-ci flathead six. A total of 82,835 were built during both production runs. The M715 Jeep Gladiator pickup eventually took the M-37's place in the military lineup.

After the War

The Dodge trucks of World War II proved so useful and sturdy that Dodge gave them an extended life in the postwar world. Civilian versions of the 3/4-ton pickups were introduced to the public for 1946 and named Power Wagons. The military-type civilian Power Wagons were sold in the United States from 1946 to 1968 (and some were even exported until the late 1970s, undoubtedly reminding assorted countries around the world just who won World War II).

DODGE CRAFTSMANSHIP LIVES RIGHT ON!

AGAIN the scene has shifted from the highways of America to the battle fronts of the world. Again Dodge Dependability of peace-time translates itself into the precision craftsmanship of war. And again the word comes back from the final testing grounds of warfare that Dodge Craftsmanship is Dependable under the most gruelling extremes of service.

DODGE MARCHES WITH THE NATION

IN THE FACTORIES: Dodge is producing motor transport vehicles field radio cars • Army reconnaissance cars • Army carry-alls ambulances • weapon carriers • gyro-compasses • aircraft parts and sub-assemblies • tank parts and sub-assemblies • anti-aircraft cannon parts and sub-assemblies • fire-fighting equipment • shells and projectiles • duralumin forgings • tank and truck steel castings Dodge makes its total effort in keeping with the total effort of the Nation.

IN THE FIELD: Four thousand merchants servicing Dodge vehicles remain at their posts of service to the essential transportation needs of the Nation. These merchants cheerfully and patriotically merge their individual efforts with the total effort of the Nation at war.

CTOBER 1942

33

The civilian Power Wagon had the 230-ci flathead six under the hood, rated at 102 horsepower at 3,600 rpm in 1948. Torque was rated at 184 lb-ft at a low 1,200 rpm.

Left
Auto company advertising during the war was almost always wrapped in patriotism, because with no product to sell the general public, the companies could only brag about their contributions to the war effort. "Dodge makes its total effort in keeping with the total effort of the Nation."

No Cadillac when it came to comfort, the Power Wagon interior had just the bare essentials necessary to get the job done. Ordering the Deluxe Cab equipment, however, netted the driver an arm rest, a sun visor, and a dome light.

Power Wagons rode on a 126-inch wheelbase, 10 inches longer than the 1/2-ton civilian pickup. The frame used seven sturdy cross-members, and the springs were comprised of multiple leafs for maximum strength. Although classified as 3/4-ton for military use, the Power Wagons were rated as 1-tons for civilian duty. They used a two-speed transfer case, and rolled on knobby 7.5x16-inch tires. The 230-ci six, rated at 94 horsepower at 3,200 rpm and 185 lb-ft torque at 1,200 rpm in 1946, was the only available engine.

Although Spartan in design, the Power Wagon could be optioned with heavy-duty accessories such as a winch, power take-off, and tow hooks. The

STILLWATER GARAGE
EMERGENCY
STILLWATER
GARAGE
DU·3·5660

trucks weren't softened much for street duty, but at least civilian Power Wagons came with items like a driver's-side sun visor, and a choice of four colors. Prices started at $1,555 for a chassis and cab, about $700 more than a standard 1/2-ton chassis and cab. The Power Wagon pickup sold for $1,627. The model designation was WDX in 1946 and 1947, although that would change frequently throughout the truck's life. In 1948, for example, when the new B-Series postwar pickups were introduced, the Power Wagon was classified as the B-1-PW.

With such a heavy-duty chassis and off-road capability, the Power Wagons were put to all manner of uses—as school buses, tow trucks, rescue vehicles, fire trucks, and countless other tasks. Dodge marketed the Power Wagons to farmers and industrial users—and with the Power Wagon's reputation, it was no hard sell.

Changes were few through the ensuing two decades, although occasionally improvements were worked in. Rubber engine mounts, a quieter engine fan and a new instrument panel helped civilize the 1951 models somewhat. The pickup box was also restyled to be more in line with the regular 1-ton pickup box, and the axles were beefed up.

The civilian Power Wagons had an 8-foot-long bed with high sides. Wide running boards connected the huge front and rear fenders. The small rear window remained a design constant throughout the Power Wagon's life. The owner of this truck has added turn signals.

As was proper for the sort of heavy-duty work the Power Wagon was called upon to perform, most of the vehicles were equipped with the optional winch, a $200 (approximately) option.

One of the few appearance changes made to the Power Wagons through the years was the bed design. As illustrated by this 1952 B-3-PW, the bed sides more closely resemble those of the standard 1/2-ton Dodge pickup. The changeover occurred in 1951, with earlier models having flatter sides and no horizontal ribs.

The heavy-duty Dodge Power Wagons were employed for a variety of uses, including as school buses in rural areas. The 1954 C-1-PW shown has been fitted with a Superior Coach body.

The Korean War-era M-37 was the last military-specific pickup produced by Dodge. Built on the World War II-type WC 3/4-ton truck mechanicals, the M-37 used unique sheet metal never shared with any civilian truck. Shown is a M-37 4x4 cargo truck.

In the mid-1950s, Dodge engineers bumped the compression ratio and upgraded the camshaft on the 230-ci engine to achieve 111 horsepower at 3,600 rpm and 198 lb-ft of torque at 1,600 rpm. The 230-ci six was retired in 1961 in favor of a 251-ci six. With a compression ratio of 7.1:1, the 251 produced 125 horsepower at 3,600 rpm and 216 lb-ft of torque at 1,600 rpm. An alternator replaced the generator in the 1960s also, giving better charging. The addition of seat belts was one of the few Power Wagon acknowledgments to the federal government's increasing influence over the automotive industry.

Of course, during this time the Power Wagons were exported as well, with Canada being an important market. As with the conventional pickups, export Power Wagons were sold with Fargo, and even DeSoto, nameplates.

By the time 1968 rolled around, U.S. Power Wagon prices had risen to $4,295, nearly twice the price of a D100 Utiline. What that extra $2,000 purchased, though, was more than just a larger truck. It purchased bragging rights, a sort of John Wayne swagger, and the knowledge that nobody, except another Power Wagon owner, had as much pickup truck.

U S ARMY 2384091

DODGE

3 Postwar Party

In the late 1940s everything automotive was reborn. After years of shortages brought on by World War II, the public was hungry for new cars and trucks and the American automakers were eager to deliver. In the immediate postwar years though, Detroit's offerings were merely reissued 1942 models, as the auto manufacturers struggled to shift from producing bombers and tanks to cars and trucks. For truck buyers, late 1947 and early 1948 was like one long Christmas, as there were all-new pickups from Dodge, Ford, Chevy, and GMC.

The new Dodge, like its competitors, was noteworthy for a general improvement in passenger comfort and convenience. The "Pilot House" cab was larger and visibility much improved thanks to a more expansive glass area. Handling was sharpened with a new steering design and an eight-inch shorter wheelbase. The pickup bed was larger as well, for increased carrying capacity.

"When a farmer buys a new Dodge 'Job-Rated' truck . . . it's a natural for long-time Dodge owners to congratulate him," print ads trumpeted. "They know . . . *from their own experience* . . . that this farmer has bought many miles of dependable and economical farm transportation. They know he's received *real* VALUE for his money."

The 1948 and 1949 trucks were given new model designations. The 1/2-tons were designated B-1-B, the 3/4-ton was B-1-C, and the 1-ton B-1-D. Later B-series trucks were labeled B-2, B-3, or B-4 depending on the model year. The B-series trucks were available with Standard, Deluxe, or Custom cabs. The Deluxe and Custom cabs offered such features as rear quarter windows and door-vent windows, with the Custom cab including such opulent luxuries as a dome light and driver's armrest.

The look and feel were all-new, although under the skin the 1948 Dodge's drivetrain largely carried over from the year before. The standard engine was still the 218-ci flathead six, rated at 95 horsepower, backed by a three-speed transmission. One-ton trucks could be ordered with a larger 230-ci six.

Another new addition to the postwar fleet was the 1-ton Route Van. The Route Van had the new

The 1948 pickups were an all-new design, with larger cabs and more rounded lines than the 1947 pickups. Deluxe cab models, like this one, had front vent windows and rear quarter-windows. The standard pickup box was painted black, although a color-matched bed was available as an extra cost option.

Although not commonly modified for street-machine duty, Dodge trucks look as nice as their Ford and Chevy contemporaries when properly modified. It's a tight fit, but a modern small-block Chrysler V-8 will fit between the frame rails of early pickups, like this modified 1950 model, without too much hacking and slashing.

1948 grille design, but had little external family resemblance to the new pickups beyond that. It was designed for delivery duty, and consequently sat low to the ground and had a tall body for easier driver ingress and egress. It rode on a short, maneuverable, 102-inch wheelbase. The Route Van also had two

The outside may have been new, but under the hood the 1948 Dodge pickups were nearly identical to the 1947 models. The 218-ci six was unchanged from the previous year, still putting out 95 horsepower at 3,600 rpm.

This stylish leaping ram hood ornament was used from 1948 to 1950. In 1951, the pickups were given a restyled front end without a hood ornament.

The Spring Special pickups of the early and mid-1950s were created to rev up truck sales after the long winter. The Spring Specials, like this 1953 model, were given flashy two-tone paint treatments. Chrome accessories were optional. *This Old Truck*

rear axles, and optional fluid drive. Route Vans were powered by the 230-ci flathead six.

After the postwar explosion of new products, Dodge's work vehicles were subject to few major changes for the next couple of years, although improvements were worked in as they were developed. The hand-operated parking brake was moved from the floor to the dash in 1950, and the three-speed shifter was moved to the steering column.

In 1951 the Dodge pickup was given a facelift, with two large, horizontal bars across the grille replacing the stacked set of three and larger parking lamps giving a more balanced appearance and greater illumination. The instrument panel was also

The 1953 pickups featured new, larger rear fenders for the bed. This same fender design was used on stepside beds for the next three decades. *This Old Truck*

The 1955 Dodge pickups, at first glance, look unchanged from 1954. But the '55s incorporated a wraparound windshield, and models like this Custom Cab (and the Custom Regal) utilized the huge, full-width rear window. The Custom Cab equipment was a $51 option. *This Old Truck*

The 1957 D100 Town Panel shared Virgil Exner's second-generation "Forward Look" styling theme introduced on all Chrysler products that year. The Town Panel had its own list of available options, including an inside spare tire carrier, a headliner, an auxiliary seat, and Custom trim level equipment. *This Old Truck*

The Sweptside D100 sat on a 116-inch wheelbase and had a Gross Vehicle Weight (GVW) of 5,100 pounds. The 1957 Sweptside had a mid-year introduction, so production was low.

redesigned, placing the gauges in front of the driver instead of in the center of the dash. Surprisingly, in 1953, the final year of the B-series pickups, Dodge introduced a host of changes and upgrades to the line. The Truck-O-Matic transmission, known as the M6 on the automobile side of the corporation, was introduced in 1953 as a $110 option. The pickup bed was redesigned, giving the vehicle larger rear fenders, and a long-bed box was offered. There were also trim and hubcap changes for the pickup, including the return of chrome headlamp and parking lamp bezels as the Korean War came to a close.

Big Changes

Improvements and styling changes, however, were no guarantee of success in the marketplace. Dodge's fortunes in the truck world steadily worsened in the early and mid-1950s, despite regular

DODGE
100

Dodge Sweptside pickups first appeared in 1957. The Sweptside utilized the rear fenders and rear bumper off a Dodge Suburban station wagon. The front fender molding on this truck is incorrect; the proper molding ran all the way to the front of the fender.

updates and improvements. One such off year was 1954, even though Dodge brought out an almost entirely new C-Series pickup. A post-Korean War recession combined with a Ford vs. Chevy struggle for truck sales bragging rights, made conditions tough for Dodge in 1954.

The new cab styling kept with the times, with such features as a one-piece windshield, and bold, open-mouthed grille. The Panel Wagon was revamped as well, with forward-leaning rear fenders and enlarged rear doors. The new enclosed truck was named the Town Panel, with the later eight-window version named the Town Wagon.

But the really big news was the addition of the "Power Dome" V-8 underhood. The overhead valve V-8 displaced 241 cubic inches, thanks to a 3 7/16x3 1/4-inch bore and stroke, and ran a 7.5:1 compression ratio. It produced 145 horsepower, a fact that Dodge wasted little time in advertising to the world. In fact, in 1954 the 241 was the most powerful V-8 offered in a light-duty pickup.

Even the base pickup was more powerful in 1954, as the 218-ci six was dropped and replaced by the 230-ci six, which produced 10 more horsepower. For 1955 Dodge punched the V-8 out to 259 cubic inches (using the same stroke, but a 3 9/16-inch bore), producing 169 horsepower in the process.

There is likely no other time in Dodge truck history when changes came so regularly as they did in the mid-to-late 1950s. Hard on the heels of the 1954 C-1 Series came the C-3-Series midway through the 1955 model year. Although at first glance these trucks look identical, the second-series pickups featured wrap-around windshields and larger rear windows. Dodge touted this as a significant safety feature. "Notice how the 'Wrap-Around' windshield wraps completely around the front corners, giving an unobstructed view to the sides as well as straight ahead," the 1955 owner's manual instructed. "Truly, the 'Wrap-Around' windshield presents an outstanding contribution to truck styling and safety." An optional $165 PowerFlite transmission replaced the Truck-O-Matic transmission during the changeover.

The Dodge pickup was given a restyled front end again for 1957, in keeping with the "Forward Look" introduced on Dodge cars. Besides the new grille design, the hood was finally hinged at the rear instead of along the center post, as with other pickups. Inside, the LoadFlite automatic transmission was given a dash-mounted, push-button shifter. The flashiest version of the 1957 pickup, though, was a new model intended to battle such upscale trucks as Chevy's Cameo Carrier and Ford's recently introduced Ranchero.

Named the Sweptside, this well-dressed 1/2-ton pickup utilized Dodge Suburban two-door station

If these fancy Sweptside taillights look like something Grandpa probably wouldn't have ordered for his farm truck, it's because he wouldn't have. The Sweptside was a city truck, designed for light hauling and cruising to the drive-in afterward.

The 100, 200, and 300 designations that denoted 1/2-ton, 3/4-ton, and 1-ton trucks, respectively, were introduced for 1957 and prominently displayed on the side.

wagon rear fenders and rear bumper, two-tone paint, special side moldings and chrome wheel covers to make its styling statement. The tailgate was a special piece modified for Sweptside use. Built by the Dodge Truck Special Equipment Group, the Sweptside cost approximately $300 to $400 more than a standard pickup, depending on options.

Sweptside instrumentation included a speedometer, oil pressure gauge, fuel gauge, ammeter, and temperature gauge. The glove box was mounted in the center of the dash on the late 1950s trucks.

Tail fins were well on their way to becoming the signature styling feature of 1950s-era automobiles, and with the Sweptside, Dodge transferred that feature to its pickup line. The Sweptside was a by-product of the realization that not every pickup spent its life hauling hay on the farm—some people wanted fancier, more comfortable pickups for less strenuous duty. The execution of the Sweptside's fender grafting was somewhat slapdash, and from some angles the body parts look as if they don't quite fit together properly. Still, it was a distinctive look. Though never a big seller when new, today the Sweptside stands out as a premier Dodge truck collectible from the 1950s. The Sweptside was produced from mid-1957 to 1959. A DeSoto version of the Sweptside, using Plymouth rear fenders, was built for export.

The Sweptside was certainly a high-profile looker, but other upgrades for 1957 were more than skin deep. These new K-Series trucks could be ordered with an even more powerful V-8 than in

Dodge truck styling went fundamentally unchanged from 1962 to early 1965. The medium-duty trucks, like this D600 dump truck, mimicked light-duty pickup styling. The W-Series 4x4 Power Wagons even used the large, flared front fenders of these larger trucks. *Texas Department of Transportation*

Trucks are put to just about every conceivable use and fitted with all manner of heavy-duty gear, as this medium-duty D600 highway department "bucket" truck illustrates. The D600 trucks were rated at 2 1/2 tons. *Texas Department of Transportation*

1956—a 315-ci, 204-horsepower stormer, the largest V-8 available in a light-duty pickup. The 315 V-8 was a $105.30 option. Dodge had already developed an enviable reputation in the truck world with the introduction of the powerful 331-ci hemi V-8 into the medium-duty truck line in 1954, and the 315 V-8 helped solidify their position as a manufacturer of trucks with hot rod hearts.

Additionally, Dodge introduced a light-duty 4x4 model that year. The heavy-duty, military-style, 1-ton Power Wagon had been around for years, but the more conventional new 1/2-ton W-100 and 3/4-ton W-200 offered four-wheel drive in a more comfortable, conventional package. The "W" designation for four-wheel drive that was introduced that year continues to denote four-wheel-drive at Dodge

Dodge's C-Series medium-duty and heavy-duty trucks were built from 1960 to 1975, with either gasoline or diesel engines. Jumping into the heavy-duty truck market was a new move for Chrysler, and the C-Series trucks did not use conventional pickup front-end styling—although the cab itself was a holdover from the medium-duty D-Series of the late 1950s. *Texas Department of Transportation*

One hates to throw around the word "legendary" too freely, but Custom Sports Specials of the 1960s were produced in such low numbers that even most rabid Mopar fans have never seen one. Fewer still were the trucks equipped with the optional 426 V-8. Custom Sports Specials, like this 1965 model, can be instantly recognized by the twin rally stripes running across the hood and cab. *Don Bunn*

to this day. All the four-wheel-drive pickups were called Power Wagons starting in 1957, a name that would stick with Dodge trucks for years.

As for exterior differences, besides the Power Wagon nameplates, the late-1950s 4x4 pickups used the flared front fenders of medium-duty Dodge trucks. Standard tires for the W100 and W200 were 7x17.5-inch. W100 four-wheel-drive pickup prices started at $2,594 (less for chassis and cab models) in 1957, almost $1,000 more than a standard D100, but still slightly less than the military-style Power Wagon. The Town Panel and Town Wagons were also offered in four-wheel drive, with prices starting at $2,865.

In 1958 Dodge pickups received yet another new face, this time with quad headlamps. The grille featured three horizontal bars running between the headlamps, with a fourth placed lower on the grille between the parking lamps. Many two-tone paint combinations were offered, and were quite popular in 1958. Quite popular, that is, among the few buyers of Dodge trucks—a rough economic recession in 1958 choked off sales of most domestic makes, and Dodge was no exception.

For 1959 Dodge introduced yet another new model with a distinctive bed, this one named the Sweptline. The Sweptline's bed dispensed with the fins of the Sweptside, offering a large, squared-off bed that ran the full width of the cab, much like today's pickups. In true 1950s fashion, the 1959 trucks received yet another new grille and, once again, the engine room was upgraded. The available

Camper Special packages were available on 3/4-ton D200 and W200 pickups, and provided the heavy-duty equipment necessary for hauling those live-in loads around the country. Shown is a 1968 advertisement detailing the assorted options available.

V-8 in 1959 displaced 318 cubic inches (not to be confused with the later 318-ci small-block V-8), and grunted out 205 horsepower and 290 lb-ft of torque. The last year of this series of trucks, the 1960 models offered few changes beyond a new mesh-type grille.

Tossing a Dart

The turning of a new decade has often marked the beginning of new styling themes among the various auto makers. Certainly the cars and trucks of the 1960s are distinct from the vehicles of the 1950s. And the styling theme established for trucks in the 1960s can be summed up in one word—square. The rounded cabs, bulging hoods, and finned fenders of the previous decade gave way to square cabs, flat hoods, and slab sides.

One of the trucks that helped establish that theme was the 1961 Dodge Dart pickup. The Dart automobile introduced for 1960 had been a great success for Dodge, and the logic of applying the Dart name to the new pickup probably seemed sound at the time, even if the tag only stuck for the first year of production. Besides the name, Dodge officials pushed other passenger car characteristics of the Dart truck, including its improved handling.

The 1961 Dart truck was lower and wider than the 1960 model, with the squared-off styling that was quickly becoming the norm in Detroit. (The WM300 Power Wagons and Town Wagons carried over with the older styling.) The one distinctive styling flair of the Dodge was a body line that dipped near the back of the bed, creating a sort of visual check mark.

The wheelbases for the various models were longer, either 114 or 122 inches for the 1/2-ton,

....BEFORE....

....AFTER....

The Deora show truck of 1967 was based on A100 mechanicals. After the Alexander brothers of Detroit were through with the Deora, it stood only 4 feet 9 inches tall and was 16 feet in length—nearly 2 feet longer and 2 feet closer to the ground than a basic A100. *Deora* is Spanish for "golden" and, appropriately, the Deora show truck was painted Candy Gold. The Hot Wheels toy version of the truck that many of us regularly sent zooming down the driveway was the same color.

compared to 108 or 116 inches in 1960. Under the skin, the revamped trucks had a new suspension system with longer springs and a "drop-center" frame that increased room in the cab.

One feature introduced in the 1961 pickups survived until the late 1980s—the new slant six engine. Inclined 30 degrees in order to provide a lower profile, the slant six was a modern overhead valve design, with a long-runner intake manifold that helped produce good torque for its size. The slant six used an alternator instead of a generator, beating Ford and Chevy to the punch. The new six was available in 170- and 225-cubic-inch displacements, rated at 101 and 140 horsepower respectively, although the 170 was only available in light-duty D100s. A 251-ci L-6 survived in the four-wheel-drive W300 and WM300.

The line of Dodge trucks introduced in 1961 enjoyed (or was cursed with, depending on your point of view) styling stability throughout the 1960s, although improvements were incorporated as they were developed. Sales were sluggish in 1961, but improved steadily in the 1960s as truck demand grew. The Dart name was dropped in 1962, and the 1961's mesh grille was replaced with a more conventional design. In 1963, Dodge introduced factory-built, four-door Crew Cab pickups, available in the D200 or W200 3/4-ton line.

The next big year was 1964, when an entirely new truck joined the D-Series haulers. Classified as the A-Series, the A100 forward-control pickup and van were intended to provide better fuel economy and battle the largest of the imported interlopers, Volkswagen. Riding on a short, 90-inch wheelbase, Dodge played follower here, as Ford, Chevy, GMC, and Volkswagen had long since introduced light-duty, forward-control pickups and light vans. But the Dodge had its own personality.

While the 1964 A100 was powered by the 170- or 225-ci slant six engines, in 1965 Dodge added the 273-ci V-8 to the option list. With a two-barrel carburetor, the 273 was rated at 174 horsepower at 3,900 rpm. The V-8 gave the Dodge an advantage the Volkswagen, Corvair, GMC, and Econoline pickups and vans couldn't match. The A100 even had a high-profile spokesman in the form of Bill "Maverick" Golden, who campaigned his 426 Hemi-powered 1965 *Little Red Wagon* wheelstanding A100 at exhibitions at drag strips across the country.

The addition of the A-Series vans and trucks to the Dodge lineup made for a somewhat crowded field, and consequently the D- and W-Series Town Wagon and Town Panels were retired after 1966. The Town Wagons had changed little through the 1960s, taking on only such items as alternators and seat belts as these improvements became available. The A-Series pickups and vans lasted through 1970, and although they never set the world on fire from a sales standpoint, they offered a preview of the minivan craze Chrysler would help ignite in the 1980s.

The A100 also provided the base for one of the most memorable show cars of the 1960s, the 1967 Dodge Deora. A collaboration between designer Harry Bradley and Larry and Mike Alexander, the Deora was built on an A100 platform at the Alexanders' Detroit customizing shop. The sleek Deora featured a unique, front-opening single door and a sharply creased and folded low-profile cab. Although the majority of the Deora was custom fabricated, parts from a variety of existing cars went

Economy-oriented, forward-control pickups and vans were produced by all of America's Big Three auto makers in the 1960s. Dodge was the last to hit the market, but upped the ante with an optional 273-ci V-8, something the others did not offer. Shown is a 1968 A100 with 318-ci V-8 and automatic transmission. The A-Series was retired after 1970. *This Old Truck*

into its creation. For example, the roof and windshield came from the rear of a 1960 Ford sedan, and the power steering box came from a Dodge Dart. The striking, gold show truck was powered by a functional 170-ci slant six engine. The Deora was a hit on the show car circuit until 1970 when it was retired.

Big Muscles and Plush Seats

As for the conventional D-Series pickups, they continued to inch along in the mid-1960s, with few fundamental changes but several improvements. One of the most radical upgrades to the Dodge line was the introduction of the Custom Sports Special option package midway through

1964. Available on D100, W100, D200, or W200 pickups, the Custom Sports Special came with bucket seats, a console, dual sun visors and armrests, and carpeting. Two sets of racing stripes across the hood and a chrome grille, bumper, and cab moldings were the major external clues that the CSS was no regular pickup.

For the engine room, the Custom Sports Special could be had with either the 225-ci slant six, the 318 V-8, or—shockingly—an optional 426-ci, big-block wedge V-8, rated at 365 horsepower at 4,800 rpm and 470 lb-ft of torque at 3,200 rpm. Ordering the 426 required purchasing a host of heavy-duty mandatory options, in keeping with the performance of the engine. A 426-powered Custom Sports Special is an exceedingly rare beast, as few were built. The Custom Sports Special option was available through 1967, although the 426 was available only in 1964 and 1965.

The seldom-ordered 426 may have been dropped after 1965, but the trend toward larger pickup engines continued. For 1967, Dodge offered the 383 in its light truck line and not just for special sports models. The 383 produced 258 horsepower and 323 lb-ft torque. A good match for the 383 was the Adventurer Package introduced for 1968 Sweptline models. It included a chrome grille and trim, sporty hubcaps, a vinyl roof, and "wall-to-wall" carpeting, with bucket seats and a center console optional. The 1968 models were further cleaned up with a new grille design.

The Adventurer package enjoyed a long life on Dodge pickups and, beginning in 1971, was expanded to include Adventurer Sport and Adventurer SE models. The move toward sportier-appearing pickups was one that gathered steam in the 1970s, and the Custom Sports Specials and Adventurers were only a taste of what was to come. Dodge had positioned itself well for the coming "factory custom" pickup wars, and in later years some of the flashiest pickups ever built would wear Dodge nameplates.

leet Dodge Adventurer, the pickup you won't want to leave when work is over.

Come on, truck owners, live a little.

re you the kind of truck owner who thinks the pickup belongs in the barn at night?
Because it isn't quite the kind of vehicle you'd care to use for socializing? Well, then, come on.
ou've got it all wrong. You haven't heard about the Dodge Adventurer, a pickup with
wo missions in life. One is to go out and do an honest day's work every day. The other is
o go along at night when you're out for fun. Because Adventurer is a good companion.
landsome, comfortable, easy to handle, willing to go with the crowd. Priced with the rest.

Adventurer is a handsome devil. Almost too handsome to be called a pickup. And its good looks are more than skin deep, more than a good-looking grille and sweeping lines from front to rear.

Here's one of the features that make Adventurer so outstanding. Optional bucket seats. Foam-padded and vinyl-trimmed to match the luxury of its standard, full wall-to-wall carpeting and the comfort of its standard Cushion-Beam Suspension that gives you a town and country ride. Add the optional 383-cubic-inch V8 engine and special-equipment air conditioning, and you'll see that Adventurer is anything but a Plain Jane pickup.

Don't buy a pickup you'll want to put in the barn with the livestock. Go Adventurer and travel first-class —day and night, weekdays and weekends. You'll never want to be without it.

Dodge Trucks CHRYSLER MOTORS CORPORATION

Dodge Adventurer... the pickup that leads a double life.

For work or play, there are 27 Dodge pickups that give you more truck per buck.

The move toward fancier trucks was in full swing in the 1960s, and Dodge did its part to create swingin' pickups. The Adventurer package debuted for 1968 with a chrome grille, flashy moldings, a vinyl top, full carpeting, and options such as bucket seats and the 383-ci V-8.

EXPRESS
TRUCK
HA6-626
Radial T/A

4 Muscle Trucks

By the early 1970s Dodge pickups were considered a bit dowdy. The square-shouldered, folded-edge look that had served so well in the 1960s had started to look old by the time Richard Nixon's second term rolled around, and Ford, Chevy, and GMC had once again set the styling tone for the market. Although sales were good in 1970 and 1971—in fact, very good—the Dodge had been wrapped in the same sheet metal for a full decade and was due for a new suit.

The new attire arrived in August 1971 for the 1972 model year. The revamped Dodge D- and W-Series pickups were sleeker and more rounded than the 1971 models, arguably even leaping a few years ahead of Ford and Chevy designs of the time. The new pickups were slightly larger, riding on 115-inch (shortbed) and 131-inch (longbed) wheelbases, compared to 114-inch and 128-inch wheelbases in 1971. Doors were longer for easier ingress and egress. Hints of the 1972 pickup's styling direction were revealed the year before in the successfully revamped B-series van, especially in the grille area. The look was clean and modern, with even the dash getting a more car-like appearance.

But the 1972 pickups weren't just dressed in new sheet metal. Dodge spent approximately $50 million developing the new trucks, which incorporated such improvements as a coil-spring independent front suspension, larger brakes, better insulation, and more creature comforts such as cruise control and an integrated air conditioning system.

The engine lineup for the pickups included the 225-ci slant six, 318-ci V-8, a 360-ci V-8, and a 400-ci big-block engine to replace the 383. Electronic ignition was offered as an option on V-8s with automatic transmissions. Model designations continued as before, with 1/2-ton trucks classified as D100, 3/4-ton trucks as D200, and 1-ton trucks as D300. Four-wheel-drive trucks carried a W designation, such as W100, W200, or W300. As with the earlier models, a four-door crew cab model was also offered.

The 1972 pickups were a fantastic success for Dodge. Production increased substantially, and market share climbed above 13 percent that year, compared to less than 10 percent the year before. Dodge kept the improvements coming, with a

The Li'l Red Express Truck package added $1,056.00 to the price of the D150 Utiline in 1978, with the package rising to $1,131.10 for 1979. The Adventurer package was a mandatory option.

Club Cab model introduced in 1973, the industry's first. The Club Cab provided an additional 18 inches of room behind the seat, and established the configuration as the truck of the future. Electronic ignition was available on all V-8s in 1973.

Dodge expanded the model range of its truck line further in 1974. In March of that year Dodge introduced the Ramcharger sport utility vehicle, while Plymouth debuted the identical Trailduster. The two were styled and sized much like Chevy's Blazer, which is to say larger than the Ford Bronco, International Scout, and Jeep Universals. All were produced with four-wheel-drive in 1974. The standard engine was the 318-ci V-8, with the 360-, 400-, and 440-ci V-8s optional.

Dodge produced 15,810 Ramchargers that first year, while Plymouth built 5,015 Traildusters. In 1975 4x2 Ramchargers and Traildusters were introduced. While being less fun to romp over trails, they were priced approximately $900 less than the 4x4 versions.

Playtime

As the 1970s progressed, a new type of truck started rolling out of Detroit's factories. The Big Four manufacturers couldn't help but notice the large number of people who were customizing their pickups, taking what were essentially four-wheeled tools and turning them into race trucks, sport trucks, low riders, and cowboy Cadillacs. Custom

The Li'l Red Express Truck used oak bed trim and flooring. This 1978 truck lacks the gold pin stripping around the wheel openings, but little else. Interiors were in either black or red vinyl.

EXPRESS
TRUCK
BFGoodrich
BFGoodrich
Radial T/A

The LRT engines were dressed up with chrome valve covers and a chrome lid for the dual-snorkel air filter assembly, plus "360 Express" graphics. Although a prototype and some engineering mules were built with the high-performance W-2 cylinder heads, the W-2s were never offered for production. The W-2 heads would have made the LRT an unparalleled hot rod truck, but could not meet the emissions standards of the day.

Li'l Red Express Trucks could be had with either a bench or bucket seats. Mandatory options with the package included power steering, the Adventurer Package, and stereo radio. A dash-mounted tach was optional. This 1978 LRT has been fitted with a 1979 steering wheel.

wheels, over-size tires, driving lights, stripe kits—all were finding their way onto America's pickups, and savvy aftermarket manufacturers were hauling away profits by the sackful.

Naturally, the automakers wondered if they could divert some of this aftermarket money to themselves by offering "factory custom" trucks. The factory customs started hitting the market in earnest in 1976 and 1977. AMC introduced their Jeep Honcho J-Series pickup in 1976, and Ford followed with their wildly-striped Free-Wheeling pickups in 1977. Chevy also brought out a Sport package for their pickups in 1977. These trucks were all distinguished by mag-type wheels, bold—if not downright gaudy—stripe schemes, usually stepside beds, lots of chrome, and plentiful interior creature comforts.

Chrysler was also a player in the factory-custom arena. Dodge called its entries in this field "Adult Toys," and launched a high-profile ad campaign around the flashy trucks. For 1977 the Adult Toys included a Macho Power Wagon, Warlock pickup, Street Van, and Four by Four Ramcharger. The Macho Power Wagon and Four by Four Ramcharger were aimed at off-roading enthusiasts, the Street Van was targeted at the burgeoning custom van market, and the Warlock was intended to impress the type of buyer who took his truck cruising on Saturday night. With gold trim, gold wheels, and wood side boards, the Warlock fit right in with the cruising scene.

Warlock colors were limited to Sunfire Metallic, Black Sunfire Metallic, Bright Red, and Medium Green. But the Warlock was not just all show and no go. Although the standard engine was the 225-ci slant six, the 318, 360, 400, and even the 220-horsepower, 440-ci V-8 all haunted the option list.

In 1978 the most famous of the Adult Toy bunch, the Li'l Red Express Truck, was introduced. The LRT was like the Warlock in some respects, but was a much more serious effort at creating a sport truck. On the outside, the Li'l Red Express Truck came with oak bed trim, Li'l Red Express Truck decals, chrome side steps, and slotted mags (15x7 wheels with GR60x15 tires up front, 15x8 wheels with LR60x15 tires on the rear). Mandatory options on the Express included power steering, LoadFlite automatic, the Adventurer package, and stereo radio. The LoadFlite was a strengthened piece, and the 3.55 gear in the rear end guaranteed smoky burnouts.

The most unusual feature of the Li'l Red Express, though, was the pair of chrome exhaust "stacks" that ascended along the back of the cab. The LRT took advantage of the less stringent emissions regulations that applied to trucks in 1978, and so featured the eye-catching stacks as part of an exhaust system that had no catalytic converters.

Rather than just use an off-the-shelf engine, the 1978 Li'l Red Express came with a unique high-performance 360-ci V-8. Designated the EH1, the LRT's 360 was a modified E58 police engine. It was equipped with such heavy-duty police parts as a windage tray, Thermoquad carburetor, and roller timing chain, plus throwbacks from the musclecar era like its 1968-spec 340 V-8 camshaft and valve springs. It was dressed with chrome valve covers and

The Li'l Red Express Trucks were all Canyon Red with gold striping. Although the 1978 models were not saddled with catalytic converters, undoubtedly the convoluted exhaust pipes leading up to the chrome stacks sapped some power. Surely, straight pipes out the back would have yielded better performance. Still, the stacks looked cool and sounded great, which for most people was enough.

The 1979 Li'l Red Express Truck can be distinguished from the 1978 version by its stacked, rectangular headlamps and flatter hood. Additionally, the 1979 versions had the same size tires front and rear, whereas the 1978 LRT had larger tires in the rear. The 1979 model is the tamer of the two, but also the most numerous.

a chrome lid for the dual-snorkel air cleaner. Horsepower was unrated by Chrysler, although 220 horsepower is a good guess.

The LRT survived into 1979, but in substantially tamer form. The 1979 LRT utilized a milder, late-model 360 camshaft, and came with catalytic converters and an assortment of new emissions plumbing underhood. Even the speedometer was federalized that year, reading only to 85 miles per hour. The tires were no longer different-sized, with the same 15x8-inch mags and LR60x15 tires front and rear.

Appearance-wise, the 1979 LRT, like all the other 1979 Dodge pickups had new, stacked rectangular headlamps, a redesigned grille, and a flatter hood. Although less powerful, the 1979 was still no wimp, and outsold the 1978 version 5,188 to 2,118.

The Li'l Red Express may have been the image leader for Dodge trucks, but it wasn't the only development of the late 1970s. In 1977 a D150 heavy 1/2-ton was introduced, which would become the base full-size pickup in 1980, replacing the D100. The growing popularity of four-wheel drive during the 1970s also led to a higher profile for Dodge's Power Wagons.

Humorist P. J. O'Rourke, in the December 1978 issue of *Car and Driver,* wrote a raucous article about the popular 4x4 machinery of the day titled "Off-Road Bash." Of the 400-cubic-inch, four-wheel-drive Power Wagon, he captured the feel of the truck perfectly: "The Dodge Power Wagon, on the other hand, was anything but refined. It's just a short-bed pickup body set on a four-wheel drive-train connected to all the engine in the world. And the Power Wagon was completely insensitive. Nothing halted it. Nothing slowed it down. It steered like a steamship. The suspension was straight off an amusement park ride. And the inertia belts were apparently designed by the Duncan Yo-Yo company. [Don] Sherman said the only way to drive it was with one hand braced against the roof, one hand on the wheel, and both feet on the accelerator. And he was right."

Retrenching

In a reversal of the automotive norm, pickups and vans were one bright spot in an otherwise gloomy decade for Chrysler. Although automotive sales were strong early in the decade, by the mid-1970s Chrysler's weakness in the marketplace was becoming apparent. The low-quality Aspen and Volare twins were a public relations disaster, and the Dodge Diplomat, Monaco, and Magnum XE weren't exactly enticing people to empty their bank accounts. At a time when the corporation was on the brink, truck sales were one of the few strong points.

Strong, that is, through 1978. In 1979 the second fuel crisis took a toll on van and truck sales in the United States and drove Chrysler to make a number of fundamental changes to its truck line. Clearly, with consumers waiting in gas lines and looking closely at fuel economy figures, big-block V-8s were on their way out. The 440- and 400-ci V-8s were dropped from pickup use for 1979. The large and thirsty Plymouth Trailduster, never as popular as its Dodge counterpart, was put to rest after 1981.

As they had done with the Dodge Colt, Chrysler turned to rebadged Mitsubishi products to boost the fuel economy of its lineup for 1979. The Dodge D50 and Plymouth Arrow pickups were powered by either a 2.0-liter four-cylinder or an optional 2.6-liter. Prices started at $4,819, and the lightweights tipped the scales at a mere 2,400 pounds. With Chrysler unable to devote engineering resources to any home-grown compact truck, the Mitsubishi twins were solid as economical fill-ins until the company could develop its own small truck—which did not happen until 1982, with the introduction of the Rampage. Even then, the D50 carried on.

The Rampage was definitely something new in the truck universe. It was a front-wheel-drive, El Camino-type hybrid, based off the Dodge 024 sport coupe. The Rampage was powered by Chrysler's 2.2-liter overhead cam (OHC) four-cylinder, which produced 84 horsepower. The Rampage had good interior room for a compact truck, and even featured a package shelf behind the

The Ramcharger had a healthy run from 1974 to 1993, but by the early 1990s the market for full-size, two-door sport utilities had dried up. The new hot setup was compact four-door sport utes, a group the Dakota-based Dodge Durango would join in 1998. Shown is a 1993 Ramcharger, the last of the breed.

seats. An interesting technical feature was a new proportioning valve for the brakes that modulated pressure to the rear drums depending on whether the bed was empty or full. Payload was only slightly above 1,100 pounds, but the Rampage was intended to be more of a sport truck than heavy hauler.

In 1982 the Rampage was available in two models, either base Rampage or Rampage Sport. The Sport had what passed for performance accoutrements at the time, such as blacked-out moldings, a passenger-side mirror, larger P195/60R14 tires and sport wheels, bucket seats, Rallye instruments, and an available stripe package that could only be described as "loud."

Motor Trend, in its June 1982 issue, compared the Rampage with a Volkswagen Rabbit pickup. They found the larger interior volume made the difference between the two. "For our money, the Rampage's extra few inches of critical legroom are worth more than the VW's extra few inches of less consequential cargo space," they wrote. *Motor Trend's* testers produced 0-60 times of 11.13 seconds, and a quarter mile of 18.06 seconds at 74.4 miles per hour for the Rampage, versus 12.97 seconds to 60 miles per hour for the VW and a quarter-mile time of 18.85 seconds.

Off-Road magazine also approved of the Rampage in their July 1982 issue. "It goes like stink and handles like a snake in tall weeds. Hey, you can even stick a load in the bed and convince everyone that you're quite the practical fellow after all." As tested, their Rampage cost $8,329.17. Curb weight came in at 2,460, pounds, and 0-60 miles per hour arrived in 10.3 seconds.

For 1983 the Rampage 2.2 supplanted the

Dodge's top heavy-duty pickup for years has been the 1-ton D350 dually club cab with the Cummins Turbo Diesel. For 1993 it had a maximum trailer weight capacity of 11,700 pounds. The Gross Vehicle Weight (GVW) rating was 10,100 pounds. The steepest axle ratio with the diesel was 4.10:1; with 5.9-liter gasoline-powered V-8, a 4.56:1 ratio was available. *Dodge Division*

Sport model. The 2.2 edition was distinguished by a non-functional hood scoop and new graphics. A 5-speed transaxle was added as standard equipment on the Rampage 2.2 model, and was optional on the base Rampage. For 1984 the Rampage received a new grille with quad headlamps, and 10 additional horsepower. Plymouth also had a version of the Rampage to sell in 1983, named the Scamp. Because only 2,129 were produced, the Scamp almost qualifies as a mythological beast. The only differences between a Rampage and a Scamp were the Plymouth grille and assorted identification.

Although a fun and sporty vehicle, the Rampage never sold well and was canceled after 1984. Total Rampage production was 27,576 vehicles over the three years of its life. The top sales year was 1982, but the truth is, some Rampages were still sitting on dealers lots for years after the truck went out of production.

Base engine in the 1993 W250 4x4 regular cab pickup was the 5.2-liter Magnum V-8, with the 5.9-liter V-8 and 5.9-liter I-6 Cummins diesel optional. A super-duty transmission oil cooler for the diesel was added to the option list in 1993, adding 2,000 pounds to the maximum trailer weight rating. *Dodge Division*

Meanwhile, on the regular pickup side, changes were evolutionary. The Adult Toys days were gone for good, though, and most of the changes were designed to improve fuel economy or emissions. The D-Series trucks were given a mild facelift in 1981, and a Miser model joined the lineup in 1982. Another moderate facelift followed in 1986, although by then the basic package was starting to feel old.

Although collectible Dodge pickups from the 1980s are few and far between, at least one rarity was produced in the late 1980s that may tempt collectors in the future. As detailed later in this book, Carroll Shelby had signed on with Chrysler in the early 1980s to produce limited runs of specialty performance vehicles. One such vehicle that came from the Shelby works was the Rod Hall signature truck, named after the famed Baja racer who had won so many races for Dodge.

Tim Pettijohn was national performance parts manager for Shelby Automobiles in the late 1980s,

Of all the drivers who have been associated with Dodge, few have brought home more glory than off-road racer Rod Hall. Hall has bagged 14 class wins at the Baja 1000 in a variety of vehicles, mostly Dodge, over a 30-year career. Through 1993 he had helped Dodge to nine off-road championships over the previous 11 years. Most of the fat years with Dodge were spent in SCORE/HDRA Class 4, where Hall piloted 800-horsepower W150s. Hall is shown here in 1990 wearing factory Dodge sponsorship. *Don Althaus*

The other big gun in Dodge's off-road arsenal was Walker Evans. Evans drove W150s in desert races, and Dakotas in stadium races. He even tried his hand in the infant NASCAR Craftsman Truck Series. Shown is hotshoe Brian Stewart in a Walker Evans desert truck in 1990. *Don Althaus*

and remembered that in 1989 the company was scheduled to build approximately 200 W150 Rod Hall signature pickups. Buyers could check the Rod Hall option at their dealership, and Dodge sent the trucks to Shelby for conversion. Shelby workers installed the lift kits, rims and tires, roll bars, graphics, and a Rod Hall dash plaque. "I think thirty-four of those snuck out," Pettijohn said. "That was a big political snafu too, because we raised the truck with a three-inch lift kit, and Chrysler was all worried about the angle of the U-joints, and product liability."

One development that almost single-handedly kept the Dodge truck line afloat through the tough economic times of the early 1990s was the introduction of the 5.9-liter Cummins Turbo Diesel six in 1989. The Cummins was truly a pickup engine with a big rig heart. Physically, it even looked like it belonged under an 18-wheeler hood. The Cummins used a huge, 150-pound, forged crankshaft, forged connecting rods, and seven main bearings. The camshaft and other components were gear-driven, eliminating chains and belts. The turbocharger was made by Holset, a subsidiary of Cummins.

Available in D250, W250, D350, and W350 pickups, the Cummins was the most powerful diesel available in a light-duty truck. With intercooler, it produced 160 horsepower at 2,500 rpm and 400 lb-ft of torque at 1,700 rpm. It was also a $3,600 to $4,000 option depending on the particular model truck it was ordered in, making the engine best suited for serious applications.

From 1979 to 1993 the Mitsubishi-built Ram 50 provided Dodge with an economical entry in the compact truck class. The smaller Rams were available as the two-wheel drive Ram 50 or four-wheel drive Power Ram, and could be adorned with various sport and luxury packages over the years. Shown is the 1990 Power Ram with the short-lived 143-horsepower V6 option. *Dodge Division*

Still, it sold in huge numbers, as people discovered it made the ideal engine for towing heavy loads. By 1993 the Cummins Turbo Diesel was ordered in some 50,000 D- and W-Series pickups. The following year saw Dodge attend to the rest of the pickup, with spectacular results.

Richard Petty returned to Chrysler in the NASCAR Craftsman Truck Series with driver Jimmy Hensley at the helm. Family members Maurice Petty worked as engine builder, with Mark Petty helping turn wrenches as a team mechanic. *Dodge Motorsport*

5 Ram Rebirth

In late 1993 the full-size Dodge pickup truck stopped becoming an afterthought. With the introduction of the 1994 Ram, Dodge reversed its slide in the full-size pickup field, established an unmistakable identity for its truck line, won over a few Brand-X converts, and made a few million dollars in the process.

How? Largely by not going with the flow. The trend in pickup design in the early 1990s was toward traditional brick-like silhouettes, but with rounded and smoothed front ends and flush glass—in other words, enough rounded corners to improve aerodynamics and, therefore, gas mileage, but not enough styling flair to scare off traditionalists.

The Dodge Ram shook up that styling conservatism. The Ram utilized a modern take on an old styling theme, with the hood rising above the fenders, 1950s style. Although the designers said they were not trying to create a deliberately nostalgic look, the retro influences were unmistakable. The massive, chrome, four-section grille gave the truck a distinctly Dodge face, and the bulging fenders contributed to the muscular look. The dramatic change was a gamble, but it worked.

As this is written, the 1994-styled Ram is still a current production truck, so it is difficult to place in a proper historical perspective. But what can be reported is the short-term effect of the new Ram on Dodge's fortunes. To start, Dodge's share of the full-size pickup market doubled, then grew some more. The Ram smashed its way into the top-10 sales list for all vehicles a couple of years after its introduction. Profits exploded, and respect for the Dodge line grew.

And, happily for Dodge, rabid Mopar fans quickly made a place in their hearts for the Ram. People raised on Super Bees and Challenger R/Ts had a hard time identifying with the front-wheel drive K-cars of the 1980s, but had no problem making the connection between their 1960s musclecars and the boldly styled, Magnum-powered Rams.

Something Different

Even before the 1994 Ram there were indications at Dodge of a willingness to try out new pickup concepts. The front-wheel-drive Rampage of 1982-1984 was one example, although one perhaps best forgotten. But for 1987, Dodge introduced the "mid-size" Dakota pickup, an idea that has proved to have some legs.

Although conventional in every way except dimensionally, the Dakota nonetheless injected a

Total production of the 1989 Shelby Dakota was small: 1490 trucks (495 white trucks with black trim, and 995 red trucks). The Shelbys were all 4x2 Dakotas with 318-ci V-8s and automatic transmissions.

bit of fresh air into the truck market. Most of the compact trucks available at the time were a tight fit for six-foot-and-above drivers, yet some people didn't need a full-size, V-8-powered pickup. The Dakota split the difference nicely. Available with either a 112- or 124-inch wheelbase (to accommodate either 6.5- or 8-foot beds), the overall length measured either 185.9 or 204.4 inches. Maximum payload capacity was 2,550 pounds. By comparison standard cab Ford Ranger wheelbases ranged from 107.9 to 113.9 inches. On a full-size Dodge D100, wheelbases ran from 115 to 131 inches.

Dakota engines split the difference between large and small as well. The base powerplant in two-

The Shelby Dakota had unique wheels, the unusual sail panel between the cab and bed, and prominent Shelby Graphics. The Dakota was the only V-8-powered, rear-wheel drive vehicle of the Chrysler/Shelby partnership.

The Shelby Dakota V-8 was Chrysler's throttle-body-injected 5.2-liter engine. Swapping the engine-driven fan for electric fans resulted in about five extra horsepower. Prominent Shelby decals left no doubt who performed the engine swap, though.

Shelby's name was embroidered in the seats of the Dakota, along with appearing on the dash plaque, bed sides, tailgate, grille, wheels, air cleaner, door sills, floor mats, steering wheel, windshield sunscreen, and I.D. tag, just in case anyone needed a reminder.

Like a carefree spring day, the Dakota convertible had a brief existence. Shown is a 1990 model, the final year of production for the soft-top pickup. No other manufacturer has rushed to follow Dodge's lead in this market niche.

wheel-drive models was Chrysler's ubiquitous 2.2-liter OHC four-cylinder; the 3.9-liter V-6 with 125 horsepower and 195 lb-ft of torque was optional. The 3.9 was essentially a 318-ci V-8 (5.2 liters) with two cylinders lopped off, allowing the use of some common parts between the two. The V-6 was standard on four-wheel-drive trucks. The 1987 Dakota was available in two models—two-wheel drive or four-wheel drive—with SE, LE, or Prospector decor packages available to spruce things up.

Although the big Ford and Chevy rigs were in no danger of getting knocked off their sales pedestals, the Dakota sold respectably, and Dodge's competitors seemed to be genuinely caught off guard by this new odd-size truck. Dodge further separated the Dakota from the common pickup herd with a steady string of specialty models and developmental improvements.

In 1989 a Club Cab was added to the lineup, along with a unique convertible model. The 1989 Dakota convertible was inspired by a booming convertible mini-truck fad in California. Young trendsetters were hacking the roofs off inexpensive Nissan, Mazda, and Toyota pickups, creating a whole new automotive niche in the process. Dodge was the only manufacturer that tried offering a factory droptop pickup to this small market.

Although an interesting concept, the Dakota convertible never really took off. One reason, some

One of the appealing features of the Ram is its modern look, a look that still manages to maintain a family resemblance to the old Dodge trucks, as the 1995 1500 and 1948 B-1-B shown here illustrate.

WRANGLER RT/S
GOODYEAR

The Ram Sport package included a body-color grille and bumper, fog lamps, a tachometer, raised white letter tires, and Sport decals. Engine choices included the 5.2-liter Magnum V-8 or 5.9-liter Magnum V-8, the latter rated at 230 horsepower and 330 lb-ft of torque. The Sport package was relatively inexpensive, priced less than $500 most years. *Mopar Muscle* magazine observers believe, was because of price. All Dakota convertibles were sold as Dakota Sports in either two-wheel drive or four-wheel drive form, making them a bit on the pricey side.

Then again, perhaps it was execution that kept Dakota convertible sales so small. The combination of mobile-home aerodynamics and soft top made wind noise a problem. As Rich Ceppos noted in a February 1989 *Car and Driver* test drive: "At 75 mph with the top up, the roar drowns out everything else. Watch the veins in your passenger's neck bulge as he attempts to shout above the gale. Watch him quit trying to talk. Watch him resort to hand signals."

The Dakota convertible only lasted two years, 1989 and 1990. It could be reasonably argued that droptop pickups weren't such a hot idea after all, but one improvement that never fails to awaken interest in pickup buyers is a V-8 engine. That improvement first arrived under Dakota hoods in 1989, although only in a limited number of trucks.

As mentioned previously, performance honcho Carroll Shelby had signed with Dodge in the early 1980s. His early efforts, such as the Dodge Shelby Charger, were mildly modified stripe-and-fat-tire cars built on Dodge assembly lines. But in the mid-1980s, he established another California assembly plant, just as he had in his Shelby Mustang days, to facilitate more serious modifications. His Omni and Charger GLHS cars of 1986 and 1987 were genuine performance cars, good for high-14-second and low-15-second quarter-mile times.

As early as 1987, Shelby's team had spotted the opportunity to perform an old-fashioned V-8 engine swap, with the Dakota playing the part of Frankenstein's monster. It wasn't until 1989, however, that the V-8 Shelby Dakota went into production. The 1989 Shelby Dakota arrived at dealers with a slightly more free-breathing version of the throttle-body-injected, 318-ci V-8 (5.2 liters) underhood, rated at 175 horsepower. The truck's looks were spruced up with a plastic sail panel between the back of the cab and the top of the bed rails, Shelby five-spoke wheels, and enough stripes and emblems that no one would miss the point.

It wasn't until 1991, the year of the Dakota's first facelift, that the regular production Dakota received the same power infusion. The 5.2-liter V-8 joined the lineup that year rated at 165 horsepower at 4,000 rpm and 250 lb-ft of torque at 2,400 rpm. In 1991 the V-8 was only available with Dodge's four-speed overdrive automatic transmission.

Although the V-8 Dakota looked good on paper, its performance in 1991 didn't live up to its promise. Quarter-mile times in the 17.0-second zone were typical. In 1992, however, Dodge came roaring out of the gate with a powerful line of revamped "Magnum" V-8s in the Dakota and Ram.

Naming the new upgraded V-8s after the old musclecar-era Magnum engines was a smart move from a marketing standpoint, but the 1992 V-8s were no primitive throwback to an earlier time. Horsepower was increased thanks to sequential multipoint fuel injection, a tuned intake manifold, high-flow exhaust manifolds, new pistons and a revised combustion chamber shape, and several other up-to-date improvements. The Magnum 5.2-liter V-8 pumped out 230 horsepower at 4,800 rpm and 280 lb-ft of torque at 3,200 rpm. The 5.9-liter (360-ci) V-8, introduced several months after the 5.2, was also good for 230 horsepower at a lower

Greenspoint
Dodge
BFGoodrich
Radial T/A

4,000 rpm, and 320 lb-ft of torque at 3,200 rpm, or 330 lb-ft in heavy-duty form. Even the 3.9-liter V-6 was given the Magnum treatment, with output raised to 180 horsepower.

The Magnum V-8s were an important step in raising the profile of Dodge trucks. The power-plants even created an unexpected phenomenon, the drag strip Dakota. The American performance world of the early 1990s was dominated by the Mustang and Camaro, but adding a 230-horse-power V-8 and 5-speed to the Dakota created a modern musclecar reminiscent of the old days. With quarter-mile times in the low 15s—and 14s easily attainable with a little tweaking—the Dakota was a viable bracket racer, and worthy heir to the R/T musclecars of yore.

Rising Tide

The Ram also benefited from the introduction of the Magnum V-8s, but Dodge's full-size hauler was clearly missing out on the pickup and sport utility boom. In 1993 Dodge accounted for only 7 percent of the full-size truck market (a market that

Although Dodge never produced a stepside 1994-and-up Ram, Special Edition Inc. of Bremen, Indiana, was happy to step in and pick up the slack with their "Ramside" beds. Made of fiberglass molded plastic composite, the bed is available on new trucks through select dealers. The Ramside beds managed to keep a large number of the stock Dodge bed pieces in use, such as the tail lamps and bumpers. The Ramside is a good example of the explosion of aftermarket pieces developed to fit the new Ram after the truck's 1994 redesign.

The 1996 Ram Indy 500 Special Edition was produced as a companion piece to the Viper GTS, which had been chosen as the official pace car for that year's race. The Indy 500 package included the blue paint with white stripes, Indy decals, unique 17-inch wheels and tires, and a special exhaust system. For 1996, 2,802 were built. *Dodge Division*

accounted for 1.2 to 1.3 million vehicles annually and $22 billion in gross annual sales), with Ford, Chevrolet, and GMC dividing up the other 93 percent. The Dodge pickup buyer had the highest median age and the lowest income of all buyers of Big-Three trucks, not a long-term formula for success. Even Toyota was getting into the big-truck arena, with their new T100 pickup. The boxy, aging Ram had clearly run its course.

Not that any of this was news to Dodge. The company had working design proposals for a redesigned truck as far back as 1987, and a plat-

Tony Raines was the first Dodge Ram driver to win in the NASCAR Craftsman Truck Series, leading 149 of 200 laps on May 24, 1997, at I-70 Speedway in Odessa, Missouri. *Dodge Motorsport*

Tony Raines' Pennzoil Ram is part of the Roehrig Motorsports stable. The big, yellow bruiser was the first Dodge to win in the NASCAR Craftsman Truck Series. *Dodge Motorsport*

The NASCAR Craftsman Trucks use essentially a Winston Cup chassis, with a 2-inch longer wheelbase, and some modifications for the truck's taller profile. The grille is the only original-equipment production part on a NASCAR Ram. The carbureted, 650 horsepower, 5.9-liter small-block V-8s run 9.5:1 compression ratios. Shown is the K-Automotive Motorsports truck of Bob Keselowski. A fixture behind the wheel of Chryslers in the ARCA stock car series, Keselowski scored his first NASCAR Craftsman Truck win on September 4, 1997, at Richmond, Virginia. It was the first Dodge victory at the track in 20 years, and the second ever for Dodge in the Craftsman Truck Series. *Dodge Motorsport*

form, code-named the Louisville Slugger, that was to be a flexible base for all manner of pickups and vans. One proposal almost given the green light was named the Phoenix and was trotted out in front of 450 full-size pickup owners and intenders in research clinics held in late 1987. The Phoenix was very Ford-like in appearance—handsome, but not very distinctive. The clinic participants rated the Phoenix better than the Ram, and equal to the Chevy, but below the Ford. Worse, the veteran truck owners judged the Phoenix to be less rugged looking than either the Ford or Chevy.

It was not the answer Dodge was looking for. A design that elicited ho-hum responses from the general public was not likely to increase Dodge's market share dramatically, or win many converts. The design team was forced to drop back and punt.

It was also during this time that a more aggressive new management team was taking power at Chrysler. Corporate executives like Robert Eaton,

After more than two decades of racing Chrysler products, "The King" Richard Petty left for Pontiac in the 1980s. His return to Chrysler came not in NASCAR's Winston Cup Series, but as a team owner in the Craftsman Truck Series. To date his team is winless, but the rising fortunes of the Dodge Ram in NASCAR's popular new series points to future Petty success. *Dodge Motorsport.*

Next page
The 1997 Dakota was available in three wheelbases, three trim levels, with nine powertrain combinations. The Dakota is built at the Dodge City plant near Warren, Michigan.

For the 1997 NASCAR Craftsman Truck Series, Roehrig Motorsport fielded two trucks, for drivers Tony Raines and Michael Dokken (shown). Dokken's crew chief was Mike Bodick, with Joey Arrington serving as engine builder. *Dodge Motorsport.*

WRANGLER RT/S
GOODYEAR

V8
WRANGLER RT/S
GOODYEAR

The Dakotas (and Rams) were helped tremendously by the introduction of the higher-powered Magnum engines in 1992. The 1997 5.2-liter Magnum, the top available engine in the Dakota, produced 230 horsepower and 300 lb-ft of torque. Other Dakota engines were the 175-horsepower, 3.9-liter V-6, and the 120-horsepower, 2.5-liter four-cylinder.

The Dakota was given a new front end and a V-8 for 1991, but the first major makeover for the popular truck arrived in 1997. Besides the baby-Ram face, the 1997 Dakota's frame was stiffened, the track widened 2 inches, wheel sizes were increased, and steering and suspension geometry were improved. Other changes, like improved door sealing, helped quiet the Dakota on the road.

The Ram 1500 SS/T replaced the Ram Indy 500 Special Edition for 1997. The SS/T was a similar package, though, and included fog lamps, 17-inch wheels, tuned exhaust, body-colored bumper and grille, and those hard-to miss stripes. Buyers had more color choices for the SS/T than the take-it-or-leave-it Indy 500 Special. *Dodge Motorsport.*

Bob Lutz, and Trevor Creed were more willing to throw the dice, styling-wise, and the Ram seemed like the ideal vehicle with which to take a few risks. What was there to lose?

The revamped Ram proposals were put before customer clinics in Fort Worth, Texas, in September 1989 and June 1990, with the final T-300 Ram clinic in December 1992. Additionally, a then-current Ram with a T-300-type front clip was briefly put before auto show audiences. As the final design took shape, so did the opinions of consumers in clinic. The exterior design evoked either "love it" or "hate it" responses, although 47 percent liked it very much. Respondents gave thumbs up to the increased interior room and rugged image and, whether they liked it or not, commented on the futuristic appearance of the T-300.

Perfect. The Dodge brain trust wanted a "quick recognition" design, one that no one would confuse with a Ford or Chevy pickup. They realized there would be little neutral ground when it came to opinions about the new truck, but understood a "love it or hate it" reaction is usually better than one of indifference.

INSIDE THE V-10

With the introduction of the 8.0-liter (488-ci) V-10 in 1994, Dodge leapfrogged the competition by a large margin. After retiring the 400- and 440-ci big-blocks in light-duty pickups after the 1978 model year, Dodge had been fighting Chevy's 454 and Ford's 460 with only pumped-up versions of the 360 small-block V-8, or the 5.9-liter Cummins turbo diesel. The V-10 instantly gave Dodge the largest, most powerful gasoline engine available in any American pickup truck, and was the only available V-10. In fact, Dodge engineers had to hold back the V-10's power output somewhat, as the transmissions were not equipped to handle torque outputs above the V-10's 450 lb-ft.

Engine type:	ohv V-10
Displacement:	488 ci (8.0 liter)
Block:	cast iron, deep skirt
Heads:	cast iron
Horsepower:	300 @ 4,000 rpm
Torque:	450 lb-ft @ 2400 rpm
compression ratio:	8.4:1
Ignition:	distributorless
Intake manifold:	aluminum
Engine weight:	800 pounds

And so the radical Ram was given the go-ahead. In the final tally, new Ram investment totaled $1.2 billion. This included the new truck itself, V-10 engine development, renovating the Dodge City plant, moving Dakota production, and building a new plant in Mexico to serve the Mexican market and build Club Cabs for the U.S. market.

The appeal of the trucks was, of course, largely due to the Ram's looks, but there were other features that set the Ram apart. It was substantially larger, inside and out, than competing Ford and Chevy trucks, especially in standard cab form. A modular storage system and huge, fold-down center console were nifty features, and the truck came standard with a driver's airbag, beating Chevy to the punch, if not Ford.

Another strong feature was Dodge's excellent engine lineup. The 3.9-liter V-6 was standard, the 5.2- and 5.9-liter V-8s optional. The popular 5.9-liter Cummins Turbo Diesel six was available in 3/4-ton and 1-ton trucks and, in the spring of 1994, the new 8.0-liter (488-ci) V-10 became available. Like the 3.9 V-6, the V-10 was built off Chrysler's V-8 architecture. It shared such parts as connecting rods with the 5.2- and 5.9-liter V-8, although not the same bore centers. With 300 horsepower at 4,000 rpm and 450 lb-ft of torque at 2,400 rpm available, the 8.0-liter V-10 was the most powerful gasoline engine available in any American pickup.

Although the V-10 had been penciled in for truck use some years before, the first production version of it debuted in the Viper sports car in 1992. While the Viper's V-10 was all-aluminum and tuned more for high-performance, the Ram's V-10 utilized a cast iron block and heads, and was set up more for stump-pulling torque. The V-10 was no dinosaur, however, with such features as a distributorless ignition system (DIS) and multipoint fuel injection helping it meet emissions and fuel economy goals.

Dodge jumped back into the sport utility market for 1998 with the Dakota-sized Durango. The 1998 Durangos were all built with four-wheel drive, with engine choices ranging from the 3.9-liter V-6 to the 5.2-liter V-8, to the 5.9-liter V-8. At 245 horsepower, the 5.9 Magnum V-8 was the most powerful engine offered in a compact sport utility. The Durango also offered a third row of seats, something normally found only in full-size utility vehicles. *Dodge Division*

AM 1500 V8
GOODYEAR
WRANGLER RT/S

The Cummins Turbo Diesel six was given its first major upgrade in 1994 as well. To meet tightening emissions requirements, the Cummins was fitted with an oxidation catalyst, and a smaller turbo with a wastegate replaced the previous unit. The Bosch rotary-injection pump was swapped for an inline pump and injectors. Dodge engineers tamed some of the turbo diesel's noise, vibration, and harshness problems, for which there was certainly room for improvement. On diesels with the manual transmission, horsepower jumped from 160 to 175.

Dodge kept the enthusiasm for the new truck high with the introduction of a Sport model in April of 1994, followed by the long-awaited Club Cab in June. As this is written, that enthusiasm shows no signs of fading. Perhaps as much as any other product in Chrysler history, the Dodge Ram introduced in late 1993 shows the value of boldness, vision, and quality execution. Who would have thought the humble Dodge pickup would be one of the key components in the turnaround of the Chrysler Corporation? That's a heavy load to haul, but not too much for the right truck.

Dodge vaulted over its three-door competition in 1998 with the introduction of the Ram Quad Cab. The Quad Cab option, the first in the industry, offered two, rear-hinged, rear doors with inside door handles. The seatbelts were integrated into the seatbacks, thus allowing rear passengers to enter without fighting a spider web of passenger restraints. Other improvements for 1998 included a new dash and new forged aluminum wheels.

Index